How to Pray for Your Family

Plus: 70 Powerful Prayers & Prophetic Declarations for Your Family's Salvation, Deliverance from Spiritual Oppressions, Spiritual Restoration and Breakthroughs

DANIEL C. OKPARA

Copyright © August 2016 by Daniel C. Okpara.

All Rights Reserved. Contents of this book may not be reproduced in any way or by any means without written consent of the publisher, with exception of brief excerpts in critical reviews and articles.

Published By:

Better Life Media.

BETTER LIFE WORLD OUTREACH CENTER.

Website: www.BetterLifeWorld.org

Email: info@betterlifeworld.org

Any scripture quotation in this book is taken from the KJV except where stated. Used by permission.

Table Of Contents.

introduction..5

Chapter One: How To Free Up Time For Personal Prayers And Family Prayers And Devotions...........10

Chapter Two: 5 Things Family Prayers And Devotion Can Help Us Achieve In The Home.........18

Chapter Three: The 7 Steps To Growing A Powerful Family Prayer Altar...39

Chapter Four: Sample Outline for Morning And Night Devotions...49

Chapter Five: Take The Family Devotion Program Further. Encourage Your Family to Wait On The Lord Once In A While...54

Chapter Six: Questions And Answers....................59

Chapter Seven: 70 Powerful Prayers And Prophetic Declarations To Bring Salvation, Deliverance,

Healing, Total Restoration And Breakthroughs to Your Family 64

How To Get In Touch With Us...............................92

About The Author..97

Daniel C. Okpara

FREE BONUS …

Download These 4 Powerful Books Today for FREE… And Take Your Relationship With God to a New Level.

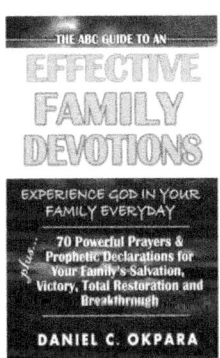

www.betterlifeworld.org/grow

Introduction

There is an urgent need to pray more for our families these days because the enemy, the devil, is on rebellion; he has released all his strength against the family system. Remember that the family was what he attacked in the beginning and was able to gain entry to destroy mankind.

Once the devil gains entry into the family, he can ruin the society with ease. The world today is failing because the family system is under serious attack of the devil.

There are so many good wishes you have for your family, but scolding, complaining and whining, planning and working is not enough to bring those wishes to come to pass. The Bible says in Proverbs 21 vs 31 that *"**The horse is made ready for the day of battle, but victory rests with the LORD.**"*

God wants you to stand in authority and claim your family's salvation, healing, deliverance and prosperity. He wants you to present your family to Him daily in prayers.

In this book, my purpose is to motivate you to bring your family together and pray for the release of the Holy Spirit. Where it's difficult to bring your family together, you can take a stand and begin to call on God for your home. Great things will begin to happen and you will see a great manifestation of God's power.

I join hands with you in prayer and decree that the force of darkness against your family is hereby destroyed in Jesus name. Together we claim victory for your family against sickness, <u>*prodigality*</u>, poverty and rebellion, in Jesus name.

I can see a great restoration for your spouse, children and entire family. In Jesus name.

Love the Lord your God with all your heart and with all your soul and with all your strength.

These commandments that I give you today are to be on your hearts. Impress them on your children. Talk about them when you sit at home and when you walk along the road, when you lie down and when you get up.

Tie them as symbols on your hands and bind them on your foreheads.

Write them on the doorframes of your houses and on your gates.

- Deuteronomy 6:5-9 (NIV)

Chapter 1: How To Free Up Time For Family Prayers And Devotions.

"There are four pillars to a happy marriage: respect one another as individuals; (give) soft answers; (practice) financial honesty; (conduct) family prayer." **- Gordon B. Hinckley**

Many Christians agree that they need to spend more time with God in their lives. But it seems that there is so much to do that this hardly gets done.

There's so much pressure on our finances, job, and social needs that we now become **fast food Christians**. Just like it happens in fast foods, you go in and just wait and take your food.

We tell God, *"Hey God, do this. I ain't got no time to wait and listen to what ya got to say. Just do it."*

And off we zoom.

After all, we chat on the go, browse on the go, check and answer mails on the go, so why can't we also pray on the go? Surely, God understands.

In fact, sometimes, we even wonder, what's the use of all these prayers? *'I can surely plan my life and get going. So why should I really be worried about praying? Does praying pay my bills and solve my problems?'*

At a public forum the other day someone asked if prayer really helps heal the sick. Unfortunately many of the respondents said it doesn't. They said that prayer only helps the people praying to feel good. But that it doesn't really do anything.

It's just so sad how deep we have gotten into unbelief and rebellion.

The truth is that prayer is beyond a *'feel good'* business. It is a very powerful spiritual trade that produces great physical results; one that we must free up time to get involved in.

If you think that you don't have enough time to pray, I'm afraid, God may not be adding another hour for you on top of the 24 hours that everyone has. I think that if you look at prayer in the following two ways you'll really begin to pray.

1. Prayers Produce Real Results.

Great changes and divine interventions do take

place when we pray with all our hearts. Your life and family will experience a great move of God when you pray.

In fact, there's none of your prayers that God will not answer. The Bible says:

> *And he spake a parable unto them to this end, that men ought always to pray, and not to faint;*
>
> *Saying,* **There was in a city a judge, which feared not God, neither regarded man:**
>
> **And there was a widow in that city; and she came unto him, saying, Avenge me of mine adversary.**
>
> **And he would not for a while: but afterward he said within**

> *himself, **Though I fear not God, nor regard man;***
>
> ***Yet because this widow troubleth me, I will avenge her, lest by her continual coming she weary me.***
>
> *And the Lord said, **Hear what the unjust judge saith.***
>
> ***And shall not God avenge his own elect, which cry day and night unto him, though he bear long with them?***
>
> ***I tell you that he will avenge them speedily. Nevertheless when the Son of man cometh, shall he find faith on the earth?***

All the prayers you have prayed before now are filling up in heaven. Your answers are guaranteed.

You should never worry or think about giving up.

---

2. Prayer Frees Up Time, It Doesn't Consume Time.

A wise man said that *"prayer doesn't consume time, it rather frees up time."*

And I agree with that.

You see, there is so much that you want to do, that's the reason there's sparsely any time to really pray, right?

Ironically, that's the more reason we need to spend more time in prayer. The Bible clearly says that not everything we want to do will bring us profit.

There is a way which seemeth right unto a man, but the end thereof are the ways of death.

- Proverbs 14:12.

There are many devices in a man's heart; nevertheless the counsel of the LORD, that shall stand.

– Proverbs 19:21

As we spend time with God, all those small plans and desires die down and we can really pursue few things and get real results.

Prayer helps us to accomplish much more than we would by just following some kind of goal setting and action plans here are there.

The above two realizations will give us the inner power to create time to fellowship with God personally and rack up our family praying times.

Chapter 2: 5 Things Family Devotion Can Help Us Achieve In The Home.

"Each family prayer, each episode of family scripture study, and each family home evening is a brushstroke on the canvas of our souls. No one event may appear to be very impressive or memorable. But just as the yellow and gold and brown strokes of paint complement each other and produce an impressive masterpiece, so our consistency in doing seemingly small things can lead to significant spiritual results."

- David A. Bednar

It is said that the family that prays together stays

together.

Family Devotions are a form of seeking the LORD with all the family involved. When administered in a loving, caring and humble manner there will be no end to the benefits, just as there is no end to the grace of God toward those who have set their hearts to seek Him.

Family Devotions help to bind marriages and families together in the love of God. Where a marriage is breaking up you will find that Family Devotions has long been buried in the home.

Family Devotions definitely increases the presence of God in the home and is a strong deterrent to the spirit of arguments, criticism, debate, and pessimism.

Family devotions will…

- Draw you closer to your spouse – increasing the unity in your marriage and giving you depth in your relationship you never thought possible.
- Draw closer to your children, building a healthy parent/child relationship founded on God's Word.
- Build your faith in God's promises as individuals and as a family.
- Allow you to communicate effectively with God, your spouse, and your children.
- Ignite a continued desire to seek God.
- Promote a healthy understanding of who God says you are.

- Increase your ability to hear what the Holy Spirit is saying to your heart.
- Build a Christ-centered confidence that cannot be destroyed.

Testimony.

After 25 years of parenting five children, Suellen Milham, the Women's Ministry Worker at Orange Evangelical Church shares the ups and downs of reading the Bible as a family - and why it's worth the effort.

She says, "If there is one thing I've learnt in my years of parenting five children, it is that God is the only one who has advice that must be listened to. However, as neither my husband nor I grew up in Christian families, we have been very grateful for those who have offered helpful suggestions on raising young disciples of Jesus that we could translate into our own family situation.

"We have worked hard at opening the Bible with our children on a regular basis for two and a half decades because God, in his word, makes it very clear that it is a responsibility and a privilege given to parents that they teach their children who God is and what he has done. How have we done it? Well, as I said, we have worked hard at it and that has meant we have tried a number of things, but I will share here what we found was workable in our family.

1. We committed to reading the Bible with our children every night

It hasn't happened every night but we don't feel

guilty about that, as life is not always that simple. We aimed to read together every night and when it was missed we pressed on and picked it up again the next evening. Some nights not everyone was there (this increased as the children got older and at times my husband would be away because of his work), but if you were home then you joined in – even if you did have mountains of things to do!

2. We kept it simple

We tried various devotion books that required some preparation and resources, but that was too hard and a lot of pressure for me. So, we simply just read the Bible. We sometimes discussed the passage and we always prayed.

Sunday nights we talked about what was learnt in Kids' Church for the little ones and the main Bible talk for the older ones and parents. On occasion we might change things up and do some Bible quizzes, but mostly we chose a book of the Bible and read it through together.

Our children's ages range over an eight-year span, but when we read the Bible everyone was encouraged to read out loud. We all read from the same translation, except our little pre-readers who would have the Big Picture Bible open in front of them at the appropriate place (we read a lot of narrative when they were small).

When our children were young we read around the table, a verse each, with the pre-readers repeating a few words at a time after mum or dad when it was their turn. Something was lost in the flow of the passage doing it this way, but it kept them all engaged with the text.

Reading aloud as a family improved their literacy but it also trained our children in the art of reading the Bible out loud and gave us some great amusement over interesting pronunciations! As they grew we switched to having one or two people read the passage.

3. We spent our time in God's word after dinner

This usually happened around the dinner table before dessert (if there was any). We have a small bookcase next to the dinner table with Bibles and a book for prayer notes in it so (most of the time) no one had the excuse of needing to leave the table to go hunting for their Bible.

4. My husband modeled leadership

It was a good thing to see the initiative for our family devotions coming from my husband. This isn't how we started, but through prayer, conversations between us and input from godly men in our church and beyond, a significant change occurred. Having him make time in God's word together a priority for his family has modelled Christian leadership to our children.

5. We had good and bad nights

We have memories of some fabulous times of fellowship with our children doing this together, and some painful memories too. Here's a few I remember:

- Having a teenager storm off.

- Watching a child put their head on their arms and go to sleep
- Having someone on the edge of their seat the whole time saying can we hurry up because they have something 'important' happening
- Trying to encourage someone who is in a bad mood to read and have them refuse
- Having dinner, a bit late, and then everyone says we shouldn't bother reading.
- Someone standing up to leave half-way through because they have another commitment outside the home.

All of these occasions can make you want to give up, but in God's strength we've pressed on…

"We have no young children anymore. We have an

eighteen-year-old in his final year of school who shares the dinner table with people who have just become grandparents. So, no 'children' and three of us at home instead of seven, but still the Bible comes out after we've eaten and we read and we pray – what a blessing!

---

1. Release God's Presence And Favor In Your Home Every Day.

When a family, in the unity of the Spirit, joins hands in prayer daily, the presence of God is continually invoked in the family; hence God's favor is activated on every aspect of the home.

It is comparable to the ark of God in the home of Obededom the Gittite that made him succeed in all that he did (2 Samuel 6:11).

John told believers that they would be in health and prosper, just as much as their soul is prospering (3John 1:2).

Praying together fortifies the presence of God in a home which guarantees the continual inflow of blessings from all corners.

The Lord replied, 'my presence will go with you and I will give you rest"

Exodus33:14

We can only possess our possessions when we travel the road of life with God's presence. With the presence of God in your home, you'll have continuous victory from the evil machinations of men and enjoy favor in times of crisis.

On the other hand, if the presence and fear of God is scarce in a home, evil works thrive. Trouble abounds from all corners. The mother is scared of the father, there is fight every day. Hatred, rebellion, adultery, immorality, bitterness and strife are the order of the day.

I challenge you, for the sake of the future generation let God's light be grown in your home today. Let us re-ignite the fire of God in our families today with the power of collective devotions, and repel every form of darkness.

2. Empower Your Family To Resist The Devil.

Be sober, be vigilant; because your adversary the devil, as a roaring lion, walketh about, seeking whom he may devour. – 1 Peter 5:8

Do we need anyone to shout before we know that terrible things are happening? More and more children are dying daily. Homes are tearing apart every minute.

The devil is trying to destroy your marriage and your children. Don't let him succeed. Your family devotion is what builds a wall of protection in the family.

The Bible says:

> *He that dwelleth in the secret place of the most High shall abide under the shadow of the Almighty.*
>
> *There shall no evil befall thee, neither shall any plague come nigh thy dwelling.*
>
> **- Psalm 91:1,10**

The more and more a home pray and fellowships together, the more they add to the wall of protection over the family. The more the children and others are empowered to resist the devil in their own lives.

3. Leave an Implanted Legacy for The Younger Ones.

"A good man leaveth an inheritance to his children's children: and the wealth of the sinner is laid up for the just."

- *Proverbs 13:22*

Business, wealth and education are great gifts we can leave for our children, but of greater value is the gift of a praying habit.

How great it feels when children look back and say:

"My mom always prayed for me. She always insisted we come together to the table and

read the Bible and pray. She never missed that. I owe her a lot."

"My dad would bless me and insist that we must pray always in the home."

There is no inheritance greater than that gift of eternal love learned from us by our children.

The Bible says that children should be trained in the way they should go, so that when they grow, they will look back and remember those ways and follow them.

Psychologists and child experts all tell us that children or younger ones learn more by observation. Try all they can to avoid it, they will continue to be influenced by the events that they observe.

When families maintain a tradition of dally

devotions, no matter how the children try to forget it as they grow into adults, the tradition remains imprinted on them. They are more likely to come back and follow the way in their nearest future.

> *No matter the level of love you show a child, without bringing him or her closer to God, you have not trained him well.*

By bringing our children closer to God, we can ultimately be justified before God that we have done our best for them and leave other aspects of their lives to God in confidence that He will take care of them.

I have noticed that the first point Satan attack in a family is their prayer altar. When he succeeds in making the family's prayer altar weak, inconsistent and scattered, he has secured access to further push his attack in that family.

God desires that all families will be fruitful and multiply in all aspects. We should endeavor to close every gate that will allow the devil gain access to cause havoc in the home (Genesis 1:28).

---

4. Prepare The Family For God's Visitation.

John Wesley was a great man of God in his life. But it was the everyday Godly devotions in his family pursued earnestly by his mum that created the very foundation of his great spiritual exploits.

As you study the story of remarkable men and women of God, you'll see visibly how one's family practice can shape someone's life and future.

Cornelius, though regarded as an infidel by the Christians of his time, was a man who did everything he could to bring his family together for spiritual instruction. Hence, when God decided to send revival to his household, the entire members were all partakers (Acts 10). If he had not developed and maintained the practice of spiritual devotion in the home, maybe he would have had it tougher explaining and involving the family members in the new move.

5. Unite The Family For Greatness

One major problem in many homes today is selfishness; or should we call it childishness; or better, unplanned division. The wife is planning her own way, the husband his own, the children their own. There is no time the family enjoys productive sharing of goals and makes joint prayer declarations of commitment and give worthy encouragement to each other.

You see, praying together in a family is one of the vital ways you can help create harmony, understanding and productive peaceful living among your family members.

> *"The fire on the altar must be kept continually burning; it must not go out.*
>
> *- Leviticus 6:12-13.*

Chapter 3: 7 Steps To Growing A Powerful Family Prayer Altar.

"Parents must bring light and truth into their homes by one family prayer, one scripture study session, one family home evening, one book read aloud, one song, and one family meal at a time. They know that the influence of righteous, conscientious, persistent, daily parenting is among the most powerful and sustaining forces for good in the world. The health of any society, the happiness of its people, their prosperity, and their peace all find common roots in the teaching of children in the home." – **L. Tom Perry**

1. Answer The Call.

"Today [while there is still opportunity] if you hear His voice,

Do not harden your heart, as when they provoked Me [in the rebellion in the desert at Meribah."

- *Hebrews 3:15 (AMP)*

There is a call of God upon your life regarding your family. God is looking up to you to lead your home into His glorious light and be the point of His blessings in your family.

Will you say to God today, *"LORD, here am I, Use me!"*

There is a great blessing reserved for everyone willing to become an instrument of divine guidance in a family. May you be the one.

"If they listen and obey God, they will be blessed with prosperity throughout their lives. All their years will be pleasant.

- Job 36:11(NLT)

Accept to be used by God to re-introduce family devotion in your home. Ask God for grace this moment and let's proceed.

Pray and say:

"O LORD my Father, give me grace, wisdom and direction to lead your WORD in my home in Jesus Name."

2. Believe God For Help.

Your family devotion is not going to be a perfect experience. There will be days when the attitude of the children will not be encouraging. There will be some days your spouse won't agree to join. But don't lose focus at such times.

It's not going to be a very perfect experience. Nonetheless God is working at all the times. Believe that He is in control and working out all things for the very good of the family.

3. Plan.

Planning is usually the first major step required in any project. So to get started, sit down and clearly think through the entire family programs and decide with your partner when the entire family can spare for morning and night devotions.

Be very clear with your decision. Is it going to be between 4:30 am to 5:15 am [in the morning] and 8:00 pm to 9:00 pm [in the night] or anything else? Choose a clear-cut time period.

In some cases, there may not be any specific time, but could be after dinner or any other time that brings the family together.

4. Inform And Carry Everyone Along.

Let everyone in your home be informed about this development and time specification. If you can, draw a ***spiritual growth time-table*** and encourage everyone concerned to take note of it and add it to their schedule.

Remember, your family devotion time is not the

time to show everyone that you can preach very well. Structure the time-table to get everyone involved, either in scripture sharing or leading in worship and praise.

5. Commit And Lead.

You are not going to be treasured because of your announcement and new time-table, rather by how serious you are with the program. You will have to provide leadership. This means that everyone will get learn from you and improve as time goes on. It also means that you will be the main driver of the program until your spouse becomes fully committed to it.

6. Make An Outline Ahead.

Try to make a sketch of how to utilize your prayer time before the time you all come together for the family devotion proper. Who will lead in songs? Who will read the Bible? Who will lead in the prayer points?

Inform ahead. This will kind of get your family members enthusiastic and follow along with you. And like you know, learn to take everyone for who they are. Don't expect them to lead like your pastor. Gradually they will grow and get better.

7. Choose Enriching Bible Study Approach.

How do you choose your Bible study methods during your family devotions?

Topical Methods.

In this method you are doing a topic by topic study. Your topic could be Holy Ghost baptism, holiness, gifts of the Spirit, divine health, deliverance, the tongue, etc.

You can systematically follow a topic day by day until your family has exhausted the topic. Then you chose another topic and locate bible references for it.

Book-By-Book Method.

This method is studying the Bible book-by-book. You could be reading from book of Romans with your family this month. You gradually take it chapter by chapter until the whole book is exhausted; then you announce a study shift to another bible book.

Low-Cut Method

In this method you really have no preplanned Bible study system. You pick this chapter today, another chapter tomorrow, and another next.

This method is also great but it doesn't lead to a rich bible study system for productive family devotion. But sometimes we could be led this way, that's alright. Always endeavor to be flexible.

Divinely Inspired Approach.

This method involves sharing scriptures that you or any member of the family has been inspired by God to share. As spiritual people we should not restrict ourselves to our paper plans. When God lays it in your heart or in the heart of anyone to read a particular chapter and learn from it, let's just follow.

Devotional Help Booklets

There are many really good devotional help booklets out there. I believe that these study aids are also great in helping us study the Bible and hear from God in our devotions. If you choose to use this approach, that's lovely.

However, growth demands that you dig into the word yourself. So even if you use any for your family or personally, you still have to practice topical bible study method or book by book study in your family devotions occasionally.

Chapter 4: Sample Outlines For Morning And Night Devotions.

"There is great power in prayer. I strongly encourage personal and family prayer, which are important in building strong families. I'm wondering if many of you parents, you couples, have lost that essential moment of kneeling together at the end of the day, just the two of you, holding hands and saying your prayers. If that has slipped away from your daily routine, may I suggest you put it back-beginning tonight!" **- M. Russell Ballard**

Now that you have decided to be answer the call for

an active family devotion in your home, let's look at a sample outline that could be very effective for a family devotion.

Remember that a cockroach cannot perch on a burning stove. If the fire in your family altar is continually burning, witches, wizards and demonic agents won't find your family a safe place to operate.

45 Minutes Prayer Outline For Morning Devotions.

This outline is designed to help you lead your family up to 45 minutes in your collective morning devotions. However, it should simply serve as a guide. If you already have a better plan, that's great. What matters is to make the meeting very effective.

Start with opening Songs	5 Minutes
Thanksgiving Prayer	5 minutes
Praise /Worship songs	5 minutes

Prayer 1: Commit the day to God	2 minutes
Prayer 2: Ask for Divine Direction	2 minutes
Prayer 3: Bind all satanic plans.	5 minutes
Prayer 4: Specifically call out needs of the family and pray.	5 minutes
Prayer 5: Pray for your church and leaders	3 minutes
Share the Word	10 minutes
Prayer 6: Pray based the word heard.	2 minutes
Thanksgiving and Announcement	2 minutes
TOTAL TIME: 46 Minutes	

1 HOUR Prayer Outline For Your Night Devotions.

Start with opening Songs	5 Mins
Prayer 1: Thanksgiving	5 Mins
Praise & Worship	5 Mins
Prayer 2: Mercy & Forgiveness	2 Mins
Prayer 3: Empowerment of the Holy Spirit	3 Mins
SHARE THE WORD	10 MINS
Questions and contributions based on the WORD shared	5 Mins

Prayer 4: Praying in line with the WORD shared	5 Mins
Next Praise and Power Worship	5 Mins
Prayer 5: Spiritual Warfare: Pray against satanic attacks, evil arrows, evil dreams, satanic plans,	5 Mins
Prayer 6: Intercession: call names of specific people, friends, family members, associates, you know need prayer coverage.	5 Mins
Prayer 7: Pray for the Church, pastors, leaders	2 Mins
Prayer 8: Pray for Your Nation:	3 Mins
Prayer 9: Anyone has prayer point?	3 Mins
Prayer 10: Thanksgiving for answered prayers	2 Mins
Benediction and Announcement	
TOTAL TIME SPENT: 65 MINS	

NOTE:

1. There is the possibility that some things were

omitted in that outline. If you know them please add them. The point is that your home/family must become a praying place.

2. Secondly, encourage members to pray in the spirit, share what God is laying in their hearts and be open for God's touch.

Chapter 5: Take The Family Devotion Program Further. Encourage Your Family To Wait On The Lord Once In A While.

"There is great power in loving, consistent, fervent family prayer. Don't deny your families this blessing. Don't allow the strength that comes from family prayer to slip away from you and your loved ones through neglect." **- John H. Groberg**

Holding a once-in-a-month general fasting and prayer with your family members can be a powerful step to spiritual growth and experiences in the home. It will help to increase spiritual stability in your home.

But they that wait upon the LORD shall renew their strength; they shall mount up with wings as eagles; they shall run, and not be weary; and they shall walk, and not faint. - **Isaiah 40:31**

When you wait on the LORD, you'll renew your strength and reinforce the grace for continuous victory.

Here is an outline that will help make this idea implementable in your home.

1. Nominate a Time in the Month:

Choose a week within a month when this will always take place. Is it the last week of the month, the first week of the month, the second? Choose the week you're led to choose. Note the days clearly. Is it going to always be last Thursdays and Fridays of the month, or something else? Specify the days clearly.

2. Inform.

Keep everyone in your family informed about that. As the date is approaching, keep announcing it.

Decide the type of fast to be done. Definitely, children will not keep up with teenagers and adults. Decide and encourage everyone to be part of it.

I have always encouraged drinking water during fasting. But if it doesn't make sense to you, don't worry about it.

Fasting is not really meant to be punishment but a way to skip one or two meals and pray more.

There is one kind of fasting you might also think about experimenting. Its fasting from 6PM – 6AM instead of 6AM-6PM. Everyone can forego their dinner in order to seek God for specific purposes. It is especially good and recommended for families.

Announce the scriptures or topics or bible books for the fast beforehand and encourage reading and praying with it individually even before your general collective prayer times.

Always keep everyone informed about the reason for the fasting. New challenges and needs will always surface each month. Keep everyone informed. Papa's business, mama's trip, Tonia's health, Bob's exams, etc. Whatever they are, make a list of everything and let your family go before God in humility.

I don't think you should cancel business, work, or school programs, because of the fasting unless there is a leading in you to do that.

Plan your prayer times well before hand. Who will lead in the opening songs? Who will share the word of exhortation? Who will lead a particular prayer point? Specify it and get them informed early informed.

If occasionally some members of your family are not able to complete the fasting, ask why, but don't judge anyone. Encourage them and let them see the reasons for this exercise especially as it will benefit them. Gradually they will improve.

Chapter 6: Question And Answers.

"A prominent judge was asked what we, as citizens of the countries of the world, could do to reduce crime and disobedience to law and to bring peace and contentment into our lives and into our nations. He thoughtfully replied, 'I would suggest a return to the old-fashioned practice of family prayer."

- Thomas S. Monson

1. "What if my wife and I belong to different

faith; she doesn't accept my kind of spiritual things in the home? How do I go about setting up a praying <u>togetherness</u>?"

Ans: "To start with, the man is the head and chief priest of the home. If anything goes wrong in your family, you are the first person to be held responsible. God will not exonerate you in any way. Remember how God held Adam responsible even though it was Eve that got deceived by the devil? So there's no excuse.

Discuss the need with your wife lovingly. This is not about **"*church*"** now. It's about the family and the future. It's about creating a tradition that will be a reference when you both are not there.

 If you do your best and she doesn't reason with you, don't try to use force, or play the man card. Love and care for her still. But don't give up on the devotion dream. Start with other members of your family; Continue to intercede privately for her salvation. God will answer your prayer.

Note that whenever she joins the praying time, that's not the time to condemn her like you've been waiting for an opportunity to strike. Love always wins over judgment…always.

Q2. "What if my husband doesn't accept spiritual things, what should I do?"

Ans. I agree that in this case we need some wisdom. Some men in some cases even insist you don't pray in their house. I know of one man who boldly told me how he warned his wife that if she prayed that night in that house, she would see death.

If your husband is really angered at praying in the home, just don't worry yourself. Keep your own devotion intact and keep praying for him. With time God will intervene and approve your faith.

Don't try to be *'preachy,'* and show how sinful the man is. Ask God for wisdom. And whenever you have the opportunity to put it across, do get him to listen to you. I believe gradually you'll win. Love always wins hatred and anger.

There are some other cases where the man is just nominal in his attitude to spiritual things, and not closed up. He may not be a part of the *'God thing'* but he doesn't stop anyone. I've seen many men who say to me, *"No, my wife can go to any church she wants. I don't disturb her. She can serve God the way she wants"*

If this is the case, then you have no problem. I've seen men who would bring their wives to church and drive away, and come back to pick them. I don't know why, but I suspect that many men ordinarily want their wives and children to be Godly.

As a woman, learn to seize the moments and ask God to help you draw your family together in great fellowships with the Almighty.

Chapter 7: 70 Powerful Prayers And Declarations To Release God's Power In Your Home.

"With the influences of evil that surround our children, can we even imagine sending them out in the morning without kneeling and humbly asking together for the Lord's protection? Or closing the day without kneeling together and acknowledging our accountability before Him and our thankfulness for His blessings? Brothers and sisters, we need to have family prayer." **- Neil L. Andersen**

1. Rebuilding The Spiritual Altar In The Home.

SCRIPTURE:

Deuteronomy 6:5-9:

Love the Lord your God with all your heart and with all your soul and with all your strength.

These commandments that I give you today are to be on your hearts. Impress them on your children. Talk about them when you sit at home and when you walk along the road, when you lie down and when you get up.

Tie them as symbols on your hands and bind them on your foreheads.

Write them on the doorframes of your houses and on your gates.

PRAYER.

1. O LORD my Father, I stand before you this day and claim my family for You in Jesus name.

2. Jehovah Almighty, I enter into a covenant to seek you in my family henceforth. Help me and guide me in my desire to be your ambassador in my family, In Jesus Glorious name.

3. Heavenly Father, I ask that your Spirit will take charge of the lives of my family members (name them) henceforth in Jesus name.

4. LORD Jesus, no one can come to You except the Father draws him. Therefore Holy Spirit, draw every member of my family to JESUS henceforth, in Jesus name. (John 6:44)

5. "It is written in Proverbs 21:1 that the heart of

man is in the hand of God. Even so, LORD, the heart of all my family members are in Your hand. O LORD, I ask that You empower everyone in my family to receive salvation and the Holy Spirit in Jesus name."

6. "Father God . . . I ask You to help each member of our family (name them) to be completely humble and gentle in our interactions with each other; and to be patient, bearing with one another's faults in love – even when we're tired, frustrated, angry, or hurt. Help us Father, to make every effort to remain united in the Spirit in this home. Please bind us together in peace. In Jesus name"

Ephesians 4:2-3

7. "Gracious God . . . help us (name your family members) to love each other fervently. Grow our

love so deep that it is able and willing to overcome and forgive a multitude of sins. In JESUS NAME."

8. O LORD, inspire a spirit of hospitality in (family member names) and enable us to cheerfully share our home with those who need a meal or a place to stay in Jesus name.

9. "O LORD, Help us to put our own needs aside and use the spiritual gifts that YOU have given us to serve one another well. In Jesus name." Romans 15:5

10. KING of kings and LORD of lords, I dedicate this home to You from today onwards. Rule and rein in this home. Be the LORD and Savior of this home. In Jesus name.

2: Praying For Salvation And Baptism Of The Holy Spirit.

SCRIPTURES:

"The Lord is not slack concerning His promise, as some count slackness, but is longsuffering toward us, not willing that any should perish but that all should come to repentance."

- 2 Peter 3:9

"This is good, and pleases God our Savior, who wants all people to be saved and to come to a knowledge of the truth."

- 1 Timothy 2:3-4

> *"Believe in the Lord Jesus and you will be saved, along with everyone in your household."*
>
> **- Acts 16:31**

PRAYERS:

1. O LORD my Father, I present my family before you. It is not your will that anyone should perish. Therefore LORD, I ask that You visit all my family members this day with your saving power in Jesus name.

2. Father, I pray, let (mention names) be convicted of your Love and be drawn to you in Jesus name.

3. Every spirit of rebellion and disobedience in the life of………………………………… I bind and cast you out into the abyss today in Jesus name.

Daniel C. Okpara

4. I command all my family members .... be set free from the power of sin right now, In Jesus name.

5. Wherever you are.................................I command you to accept Jesus as your Lord and personal savior. Receive a meek and humble spirit right now, In Jesus name.

6. Holy Spirit of God, take over my family from today. Take over the life of (mention names) and establish them in the knowledge of Christ. In Jesus name.

7. O LORD my Father, give ....the power and wisdom to resist sin and temptations henceforth, in Jesus name.

8. O LORD, baptize (mention names) wth the Holy

Spirit. Let Your power from above descend on him wherever he is right now. In Jesus name.

9. Every spirit of resistance, I cast you out of (mention names) right now, in Jesus name.

10. LORD, I thank You for visiting (mention names) with Your saving power, In Jesus name.

3. Prayer Of Cleansing The Home.

SCIPTURE:

"If my people, who are called by my name, will humble themselves and pray and seek my face and turn from their wicked ways, then I will hear from heaven, and I will forgive their sin and will heal their land. – **2 Chronicles** **7:14**

PRAYER:

1. *"Heavenly Father, I come to You on behalf of my family. I ask for forgiveness in any way we have sinned against You. Forgive us in Jesus name.*

2. *LORD, Let the Blood of Jesus flow into the roots*

of my family right now and cleanse us from all forms of unrighteousness, In Jesus name.

3. LORD I pray, let every root of sin and rebellion be uprooted in this family, in Jesus name.

4. Every evil seed planted in this family (name it), I command you to die by fire, in Jesus name.

5. O LORD, whatever has been programmed to cause discord and confusion in this family, I command them to be destroyed henceforth, In Jesus name.

5. As I anoint this house, I decree a total cleansing from evil, In Jesus name.

6. LORD, empower us to walk in obedience from now onwards. In the name of Jesus Christ. .

7. I decree henceforth that we shall never ever

labor in vein. We receive the grace of righteousness in this family in Jesus name.

8. I pray LORD, from now onwards, cause us to rely on the strength and energy that You provide alone. I pray that **everything we do within this family unit will bring you glory** *through the One who lives in us – your Son, Jesus Christ. 1 Peter 4:8-11. In Jesus name.*

9. Every enemy of this family, I command you to be disgraced in Jesus name.

10. May the evil they have planned against us be upon them, for it is written, 'He has brought back their wickedness upon them And will destroy them in their evil; The LORD our God will destroy them. In Jesus name.

4: Prayer For Deliverance From Demonic Attacks And Oppressions In The Family.

SCRIPTURES:

No weapon that is formed against thee shall prosper; and every tongue that shall rise against thee in judgment thou shalt condemn. This is the heritage of the servants of the LORD, and their righteousness is of me, saith the LORD. – **Isaiah 54:17.**

1. "O LORD my Father, today, I dethrone every evil throne that has been raised against my family in Jesus name.

2. Every force of wickedness working against any member of this family be destroyed in Jesus name.

3. Every power assigned to cause rebellion and destruction in this home, perish by fire right now, in Jesus name.

4. Henceforth, LORD, I loose any member of this family under the bondage of the devil; I command them to regain their freedom in all points of their lives. In Jesus name.

5. Every negative statement and curse against my family is destroyed right now in Jesus name.

6. I replace any curse working against us before now with the blessings of God. Where the enemy had decreed death, I decree life. Where they decreed sickness, I decree healing and divine health. Where they decreed failure and stagnation, I decree prosperity and divine favor, In Jesus name.

7. I condemn every tongue speaking evil against my life and my family. I bring them to judgment today. I command them to tear apart in Jesus name.

8. Every man or woman sitting down to hold a meeting against me and my family, wherever they are, LORD, I command fire from heaven to scatter them in Jesus name

9. I detach myself and all members of my family from every negative attachment that is not bringing glory to God. By the Blood of Jesus, I decree that we have victory; we have been delivered to walk in righteousness. In Jesus name.

5: **Praying For Divine Guidance And Favor.**

SCRIPTURES:

Psalms 32:8 - *I will instruct thee and teach thee in the way which thou shalt go: I will guide thee with mine eye.*

Proverbs 3:5-6 - *Trust in the LORD with all thine heart; and lean not unto thine own understanding. In all thy ways acknowledge him, and he shall direct thy paths.*

John 16:13 - *Howbeit when he, the Spirit of truth, is come, he will guide you into all truth: for he shall not speak of himself; but whatsoever he* shall hear, [that] shall he speak: and he will shew you things to come.

Isaiah 30:21 - *And thine ears shall hear a word behind thee, saying, This [is] the way, walk ye in it, when ye turn to the right hand, and when ye turn to the left.*

James 1:5-6 - *If any of you lack wisdom, let him ask of God, that giveth to all [men] liberally, and upbraideth not; and it shall be given him*

PRAYERS:

1. "O LORD, I thank you because it is Your desire to guide us. Thank You because You have given us the

Holy Spirit to guide and lead us into all truth. May you be praised forever and ever in Jesus name.

2. O LORD, my Father, there are many desires and plans in our hearts. But only Your counsel shall stand. I therefore surrender all our plans before You. Let the Holy Spirit guide us in Jesus name.

3. Cause us to lose interest in any project and plan that is a spiritual trap, that is not part of your plans for our lives in Jesus name.

4. I ask for wisdom for my life and family. Teach us to walk in the path ordained for us...In Jesus Name.

5. Whatever is blocking our spiritual ears from hearing from You, LORD, Let it be destroyed in Jesus name.

6. Holy Spirit, I invite YOU into my life and family. Come and be our Guide. Come and be our teacher. Come and be our instructor in Jesus name.

7. O LORD, I speak favor into this family in Jesus name. According to your Word in **Psalms 5:12**, LORD, You will bless us and surround us with favor as a shield. Thank You because your WORD is yea and amen. We are walking in divine favor. In Jesus name

8. Almighty Father, You do not withhold good things from your children according to Psalm 84:11. Everything that makes life great is our portion. In Jesus name.

9. Men and women are working for our good henceforth. My Family is experiencing favor all around us in Jesus name.

10. Thank YOU, Abba Father, You have risen to have mercy upon us. For this is the time to favor us. Yea, this is our set time, In Jesus name. (Psalms 102:13)

6: **Praying For Divine Protection.**
SCRIPTURES:

Psalm 91:1-12

> ***2 Thessalonians 3:3*** *- But the Lord is faithful, who shall establish you, and keep you from evil.*

> ***2 Timothy 4:18*** *- And the Lord shall deliver me from every evil work, and will preserve [me] unto his heavenly kingdom: to whom [be] glory for ever and ever. Amen.*

PRAYERS AND PROPHETIC DECLARATIONS:

1. *Because we dwell in the secret place of the most High, we shall abide under the shadow of the Almighty. In Jesus name*

2. *We will say of the LORD, He is our refuge and my fortress: our God; in him will we trust. Surely he shall deliver us from the snare of the fowler, and from the noisome pestilence. In Jesus name.*

3. *God will cover us with his feathers, and under his wings shall we find refuge. God's truth shall be our shield and buckler. In Jesus name.*

5. *We shall not be afraid for the terror by night; nor for the arrow that flies by day; Nor for the pestilence that walks in darkness; nor for the*

destruction that happens in the afternoon.

6. A thousand shall fall at our side, and ten thousand at our right hand; but it shall not come near us. In Jesus name.

7. Because we have made the LORD our refuge and fortress, only with our eyes shall we behold and see the reward of the wicked. There shall no evil befall us, neither shall any disease come near our house. In Jesus name.

8. God will give his angels charge over us to keep us in all your ways. They shall bear us up in [their] hands; we will not dash our foot against a stone. In Jesus name.

9. We shall tread upon the lion and serpent: We will trample the dragons under our feet. In Jesus name.

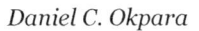

10. God will deliver us and set us on high and satisfy us with long life, in Jesus name.

ADAPTED FROM PSAL 91.

7: Praying For Divine Provision.

SCRIPTURES:

Matthew 6:26 - Behold the fowls of the air: for they sow not, neither do they reap, nor gather into barns; yet your heavenly Father feedeth them. Are ye not much better than they?

---

2 Peter 1:3 - According as his divine power hath given unto us all things that [pertain] unto life and godliness, through the knowledge of him that hath called us to glory and virtue:

Philippians 4:19 - *But my God shall supply all your need according to his riches in glory by Christ Jesus.*

Philippians 4:19 - *But my God shall supply all your need according to his riches in glory by Christ Jesus.*

PRAYERS:

1. O LORD, my God, because you are our shepherd, we shall not be in want. You will lead us in green pastures. In Jesus name.

2. My Family shall have all sufficiency at all times. We shall share with many and not borrow. In Jesus name.

3. Every spirit of worry and anxiety, I bind you and cast you into abyss. Loose your grips from our

lives in Jesus name.

4. We are not anxious for anything, because God is our support. Our needs are met supernaturally everyday in Jesus name.

5. If God takes care of the birds of the air, how much more me and my family. God is taking care of us. We have all that we need at all times. Doors and supplies are open before us. We have abundance in Christ Jesus, In Jesus name.

6. We are confident that God who started a good work in us will bring it unto perfection **(Philippians 1:6)**. We shall never be stranded. We are moving forward and glorifying God. In Jesus name.

7. LORD, I ask that You baptize us with the spirit

of contentment. Let the power of greed be destroyed in our lives and family in Jesus name.

8. God's thoughts and plans for me and my family is to have great peace and a great future. I therefore decree that our tomorrow is secured . We have peace on all sides, In Jesus name.

9. When others are complaining for being cast down, we shall be saying there is a lifting up. This is the Word of God (Job 22:29). And it is the heritage of this family.

10. Almighty Father, thank you. You are forever exalted in my life and family, In Jesus name.

Other Books from The Same Author

1. Prayer Retreat: 21 Days Devotional With 500 Powerful Prayers & Declarations to Destroy Stubborn Demonic Problems, Dislodge Every Spiritual Wickedness Against Your Life and Release Your Detained Blessings

2. HEALING PRAYERS & CONFESSIONS: Powerful Daily Meditations, Prayers and Declarations for Total Healing and Divine Health.

3. 200 Violent Prayers for Deliverance, Healing and Financial Breakthrough.

4. Hearing God's Voice in Painful Moments: 21 Days Bible Meditations and Prayers to Bring Comfort, Strength and Healing When Grieving for the Loss of Someone You Love.

5. Healing Prayers: 30 Powerful Prophetic Prayers that Brings Healing and Empower You to Walk in Divine Health.

6. Healing WORDS: 55 Powerful Daily Confessions &

Declarations to Activate Your Healing & Walk in Divine Health: Strong Decrees That Invoke Healing for You & Your Loved Ones

7. Prayers That Break Curses and Spells and Release Favors and Breakthroughs.

8. 7 Days Fasting With 120 Powerful Night Prayers for Personal Deliverance and Breakthrough.

9. 100 Powerful Prayers for Your Teenagers: Powerful Promises and Prayers to Let God Take Control of Your Teenagers & Get Them to Experience Love & Fulfillment

10. How to Pray for Your Children Everyday: + 75 Powerful Prayers & Prophetic Declarations to Use and Pray for Your Children's Salvation, Future, Health, Education, Career, Relationship, Protection, etc

11. How to Pray for Your Family: + 70 Powerful Prayers and Prophetic Declarations for Your Family's Salvation, Healing, Victory, Breakthrough & Total Restoration.

12. Daily Prayer Guide: A Practical Guide to Praying and Getting Results – Learn How to Develop a Powerful Personal Prayer Life

13. Make Him Respect You: 31 Relationship Advice for Women to Make their Men Respect Them.

14. How to Cast Out Demons from Your Home, Office and Property: 100 Powerful Prayers to Cleanse Your Home, Office, Land & Property from Demonic Attacks

15. Praying Through the Book of Psalms: Most Powerful Psalms and Powerful Prayers & Declarations for Every Situation: Birthday, Christmas, Business Ideas, Breakthrough, Deliverance, Healing, Comfort, Exams, Decision Making, Grief, and Many More.

16. STUDENTS' PRAYER BOOK: Powerful Motivation & Guide for Students & Anyone Preparing to Write Exams: Plus 10 Days of Powerful Prayers for Wisdom, Favor, Protection & Success in Studies, Exams & Life.

17. How to Pray and Receive Financial Miracle: Powerful Prayers for Financial Miracles, Business and Career Breakthrough

18. Prayers to Destroy Witchcraft Attacks Against Your Life & Family and Release Your Blessings

19. Deliverance from Marine Spirits: Powerful Prayers to Overcome Marine Spirits – Spirit Husbands and Spirit Wives – Permanently

20. Deliverance From Python Spirit: Powerful Prayers to Defeat the Python Spirit – Spirit of Lies, Deceptions and Oppression.

Get In Touch With Us

Thank you for reading this book. I believe you have been blessed. Please consider giving this book a review on Amazon.

Here are other titles that will also bless your life:

www.amazon.com/author/danielokpara

I also invite you to checkout our website at www.BetterLifeWorld.org and consider joining our newsletter, which we send out once in a while with great tips, testimonies and revelations from God's Word for a victorious living.

Feel free to drop us your prayer request. We will join faith with you and God's power will be released in your life and the issue in question.

About The Author

Brother Daniel Okpara brings you the message of hope, healing, deliverance and total restoration. A humble minister and teacher of God's Word, businessman and lecturer, he is a strong believer that with God all things are possible.

Yes. The challenges of life are real, but with faith, you will surely win. Your health, relationship, and finances can be restored by God's grace and power, no matter how bad things are at the moment.

He is the international director of Better Life World Outreach Center, a non-denominational, evangelism ministry committed to:

- Taking the entire Gospel to the entire world, from village to village, town to town, city to city, state to state and nation to nation, in partnership with established churches.

- Training ministers, evangelists, and missionaries and providing them with tools, resources and impartation for the end-time assignment.

- Restoring the evangelism fire in the body of Christ through church workers' revivals and training.

- Producing evangelism materials and tools (films, tracts, books, devotionals) for rural, screen and world evangelism.

He is the host of Better Life Today, a Monthly non-denominational fellowship meeting that receives hundreds of people each month for spiritual fellowship, ministrations, prayers, business workshops, worship, healing, miracles and diverse encounters with God. He also co-hosts a popular radio and TV program, "Keys to a Better Life", aired on over

10 radio and TV stations across the country. Daniel Okpara holds a Master's Degree in Theology from Cornerstone Christian University. A strong believer in hard work, continuous learning and prosperity by value creation, he is also the founder of Integrity Assets Ltd, a real estate and IT consulting company that manages an eCommerce startup and consults for companies on Digital Marketing.

He has authored over 50 books and manuals on healing, prayer, Marriage and relationship, Investment, Doing business and Digital Marketing.

He is married to Prophetess Doris Okpara, his prayer warrior, best friend, ministry partner, and they are blessed with a boy and a girl, Isaac and Annabel.

NOTES

Printed in Great Britain
by Amazon